FORMATION

Other books by Matt Bialer

Radius
Wing of Light
Already Here
Ark
Black Powder
Bridge
Tell Them What I Saw
He Walks On All Fours
Kings of Men
Ascent
Frequencies

FORMATION

Matt Bialer

WEIRDO MAGNET

Formation
by Matt Bialer

First published in 2016 by
WEIRDO C ~ MAGNET
an imprint of Leaky Boot Press
http://www.leakyboot.com

ISBN: 978-1-909849-30-3

FORMATION

To Lenora and Izzy

Thank you so much
Jim Goddard and Seb Doubinsky.

And I also want to thank
Jerry Wilson and Matthew Lippman.

They don't have a name
Until today

When he has the sighting

They are here

They have been here a long time

And now they have a name

June 24, 1947

32 year old businessman
Kenneth Arnold

Owner of
Great Western Fire Control Company

Sale and installation
Of firefighting equipment

Business takes him
Through five western states

A territory he has covered
For almost a decade

Business is good

Bought his own
CallAir A-2 mountain plane

For five thousand dollars

FORMATION

And for a kid
From Sudeka, Minnesota

Later by way
Of Minot, North Dakota

Represents
Fulfillment of a dream

They don't have a name
Until today

When he has the sighting

First ride
In an airplane

When he was just 14

Heavier than air
Powered craft

Still in early days

World War 1
A boon to the industry

Military biplanes
Curtis JN4s

Affectionately called Jennies

Flood the surplus market

End of war
Thousands of newly trained pilots

Steady work
In aviation

Mail routes

And two new
Interbred aerial innovations

Are born

The flying circus

And the barnstormers

Pilots
With their own planes

Travel from
One rural town to another

Offer paid rides
To the locals

Landing sites
Are farm pastures

Adjacent to a barn

Legendary Earl Vance
Barnstormer

**Time Flies
Why don't you?**

Fly where you are going

Airplane rides
One dollar a minute

25 mile minimum

**Intended For People
Who Value Their Time**

FORMATION

Exhibition flights
Public gatherings

Parachute jumps

Aerial advertising

Flight instruction

Value their time

Earl Vance
Lands on a hill

Just north
Of Minot, North Dakota

14 year old
Kenneth Arnold

Wide-eyed

Takes his first ride
In an airplane

I'll never forget that day
Greatest thrill of my life

Fulfillment of a dream

They don't have a name
Until today

When he has the sighting

Fly Where You Are Going

Early morning
June 24th, 1947

Just finishes
Installing firefighting equipment

Central Air Service
Chehalis, Washington

Chats with
Herb Critzer

Chief pilot
For Central Air Service

About among other things
Possible location

Of twin engine C-46 Marine transport plane

Been missing
Since December 10, 1946

32 men aboard

Left San Diego
10:31 in the morning

Formation of six planes

Cruising altitude
180 miles per hour

Bad weather over Oregon

Worsens

Four of the six planes
Abort their flights

Land in Portland

FORMATION

Fifth plane
Somehow makes it

All the way
To Point Naval Station
At Seattle

By 4:13 pm
The sixth plane

In severe distress

Badly off course

Freezing fog

Pounding sleet

Brutal Northwestern storm

Severe distress

The plane
And 32 souls aboard

Has vanished

Vanished

They don't have a name
Until today

When he has the sighting

Likely loss of life
Represents greatest ever

In US aviation history

Parents and relatives
Of 32 marines

Form reward pool

Several thousand dollars
For plane's discovery

We haven't given up hope

The plane may be down
In isolated forest country

Help us

Help us find our boys

Reward offered

To all fliers,
Hunters, woodsmen

Help us

Help us find our boys

You will be rewarded

Rewarded

More than $4,000
In deposit

Gray's Harbor National Bank
Aberdeen

The latest report
Among hundreds received

George Stoker of Richland

FORMATION

120 miles from Mount Adama

Says he saw
A strange glow

Direction of the mountain
The day after the plane disappeared

A strange glow

They don't have a name
Until today

When he has the sighting

They are here

Reward upped
To $5,000

A Ford Deluxe 4 door sedan
Can be bought
For under $3,000

Four bedroom house
In Seattle
$6,000

For many it is not
The grief of the families

But the size
Of the reward

Fulfillment of a dream

Belief that
The wreckage

And the gruesome cargo
Of 32 bodies

Won't be located

Until the snow
Blanketing the mountain country

Melts

Fulfillment of a dream

Wait until summer

The thaw

Mountaineers
Hikers

Focal point of search

Western slope
Of Mount Rainer

A strange glow

Air maps

Aerial photos
Of likely region

Suspicious bumps

Irregularities

Find the plane

Promise of riches

Spring gives way
To summer

FORMATION

Fulfillment of a dream

The snow is melting

Find the plane

They don't have a name
Until today

When he has the sighting

32 year old businessman
Kenneth Arnold

Smells an opportunity

Decides to spend
Some extra time in the air

Vicinity of Mount Rainer

Attempt to locate wreckage

Fulfillment of a dream

Takes off
From Chehalis

Searches

Searches for a good hour

Nothing

Not finding anything

Promise of riches

Turns east
Toward his next destination

Yakima, Washington

Oh well, I gave it a good try

Now over Mineral

22 miles
West-southwest of Mount Rainer

The air so smooth today

So smooth

And clear

A pleasure to fly

I'm a lucky man

Wife and two girls

One of them a little ballerina

Swan Queen Odette
Swan Lake

And I get to fly

A pleasure to fly

Trims out
His airplane

Direction Yakima

Trims out

Observes sky
And terrain

FORMATION

A DC-4
Off to the left

And rear of him

Approximately
15 miles distance

14,000 elevation

Sky and air
Clear as crystal

Makes 180 degree turn

Over Mineral

Altitude 9200 feet

A tremendously bright flash

Lights up the surface
Of his aircraft

Tremendously bright flash

Reflected on his plane

Startles him

*Am I too close
To another aircraft?*

Startles him

Next 20 to 30 seconds

Urgently searches sky
All around

Sides

Above and below him

Where did that flash come from?

Where?

The only other plane

Was the DC-4
To his left

San Francisco to Seattle run

But it's gone

Gone

Maybe some lieutenant
In a P-51

Just gave me a buzz
Across my nose

That it was the sun
Reflecting off his wings

Off his wings

As he passed

Caused the flash

Tries to collect his thoughts

A tremendously bright flash

Lights up the surface
Of his airplane

Tremendously bright flash

FORMATION

Again

So brilliant

Lights up whole cockpit
Whole cockpit

Like a welder's arc light

A welder's arc light

What is happening?

This time he sees direction
From which it came

Observes to his left

To the north

Formation

Of very bright objects

Coming from vicinity
Of Mount Baker

Flying very close
To the mountain top

Incredible speed

Like a welder's arc light

What are those?

A chain
Of peculiar looking aircraft

Nine

They don't have a name
Until today

They don't have a name

Nine peculiar looking aircraft

Flying from north
To south

9500 foot elevation

Direction of 170 degrees

He can't make out their shapes

Their shapes

Over 50 miles away

But they're large

At impossible speed

Impossible

They don't have a name

Must be
Some sort of jets

Military jets

In group count
That he has used

In counting cattle
And game from the air

They number nine

FORMATION

Flying diagonally

Echelon formation

Larger gap
In their echelon

Between the first four
And last five

Does not see any tails
On them

Does not see any tails

But they're jets

Must be new

Military is artful
In knowledge and use of camouflage

Observes outlines

As they flip
And flash against the snow

And the sky

Two or three of them
Every few seconds

Dip or shift slightly

Enough for sun
To strike them

At an angle

That reflects
On his plane

Lights up whole cockpit

Whole cockpit

Since the formation
Of craft

At almost right angles

To him

Traveling north to south

In excellent position
To clock their speed

Two definite points
To use as markers

Mount Rainer
And Mount Adams

47 miles to the south

Air is so clear
Easy to determine

Approximate shape
And size

Second hand
Of 8 day clock

On his instrument panel
1 minute to 3 pm

FORMATION

Fly like many times
He has observed geese

Diagonal
Chain-like line

As if linked together

Swerve in and out
Of high mountain peaks

Turns his aircraft sideways

Opens his window

To get better view

I'm not seeing things

Not flying
Like any formation I know

Forget the reward money

The echelon formation

Backward from that
Practiced by Army Air Force

Definite formation

But erratically

Like speed boats
On rough water

The tail of a Chinese kite
Blowing in the wind

Like a saucer
If you skipped it across the water

Like a saucer

They don't have a name
Until today

When he has the sighting

Like a saucer

Flutter and sail

Tip their wings

Very bright

Blue-white flashes
Emit from the center

Of their surfaces

And then he gets closer

Blue-white flashes emit
From the center

Of their surfaces

They are here

They have been here a long time

And now they have a name

Blue- white flashes emit
From the center

Of their surfaces

FORMATION

Similar in pulsation
And rhythm and beating

Of the human heart

★★

I swear I'm not lying
I swear it

Three days earlier
June 21, 1947

Seaman Harold Dahl
In his boat

The North Queen

Patrolling the east bay
Of Maury Island

Scavenging for valuable
Drifting logs

That he can resell

Uninhabited island

Three miles from Tacoma

On board
Two crewmen

His 15 year old son

And his dog Chip

Looks up
From the wheel of his boat

Notices
Six very large

Doughnut shaped craft

2000 feet
Above the water

Almost directly overhead

Are those balloons?

What are they?

What are they?

I swear I'm not lying
I swear it

Chip is barking

Five of the strange craft

Circle

Very slowly

Around sixth one

Stationary

In the center
Of the formation

Stationary
But wobbling

Losing altitude

Falling rapidly

FORMATION

Some sort of trouble

Some sort of trouble

In the center
Of the formation

I swear I'm not lying
I swear it

What are they?

What are they?

The other aircraft

Stay at distance

Of about 200 feet
Above the center one

As if following
The center one down

Come to rest
Almost directly overhead

500 feet about the water

What are they?

What are they?

All on board
Watching

Chip going berserk

Unsure
Of what is going on

What it is
That they are seeing

No motors

Propellers

Any visible signs
Of propulsion

They make no sound

No sound

One hundred feet
In diameter

Each has a hole
In the center

25 feet in diameter

Shell-like
Gold silver

Their surfaces
Seem of metal

Metal

Appear to be burled

When light
Shines on them

Through the clouds

They are brilliant

Not one brilliance

FORMATION

But of many brilliances

Many brilliances

Like the dashboard
Of a brand new Buick

I swear I'm not lying
I swear it

Large portholes
Equally spaced

Around the outside
Of their donut exterior

Five to six feet
In diameter

Dark circular continuous windows

On the inside
And bottom

Of their donut shapes

They are brilliant

Not one brilliance

But of many brilliances

The center one

It's going to crash!

It's going to crash!

They pull
The North Queen

To the beach

Get out harbor patrol camera

Snap 4 photographs

Of these balloons

Balloons

Center balloon-like aircraft
Remains stationary

500 feet from the water

Other five keep
Circling over it

Circling over it

What are they?

What are they?

After six minutes
Of the craft

From the circling formation

Leaves its place

Lowers itself

Right next
To the stationary one

Appears to touch it

Touch it

FORMATION

Stays stationary
Next to it

What are they doing?

Let's get out here!

Appears to be giving
Some kind of assistance

They are brilliant

Not one brilliance

But of many brilliances

Many brilliances

Three or four minutes

A dull thud

Like an underground explosion

Or a giant
Stumping his heel

On damp ground

Center aircraft

Begins spewing forth

What seems like

Confetti

Or thousands
Of newspapers

From somewhere
Inside its center

I swear I'm not lying
I swear it

Confetti

Newspapers

A white type
Of very light weight metal

Flutters to earth

Flutters

Lights up the bay

Hail on them

In the bay

Over the beach

And then
A darker type metal

Looks similar
To lava rock

Fragments

A darker color

Hitting the beach

Fragments

Let's get out of here!

FORMATION

Let's get out of here!

Molten fragments

When they hit the bay

Steam rises from the water

★★

They don't have a name
Until today

When he has the sighting

They are here

They have been here a long time

And now they have a name

4 pm

Kenneth Arnold
Lands at Yakima, Washington

Straight to Al Baxter

General Manager
Central Aircraft

He's a rational fellow

Asks to see him in private

Drops what he is doing

Meet in his private office

Have a smoke

Chesterfields

Relates the story
Of his observation

Draws pictures

Of what he saw

Maps

Baxter looks at him

Squints

Puzzled

You saw something
But I am sure there's an explanation

Calls in several
Of his flight pilots,
Helicopter instructors

To listen to his story

Ahh, it's just a bunch
Of guided missiles
From Moses Lake

They don't have a name
Until today

When he has the sighting

Takes off
For Pendleton, Oregon

They number nine

FORMATION

Flying diagonally

Echelon formation

Remembers

He forgot to mention

That one of the craft

Looked different
From the rest

Darker

Different shape

Like a crescent

A crescent

A tremendously bright flash

Lights up the surface
Of his aircraft

Lights up whole cockpit

Like a welder's arc light

Whole cockpit

While flying to Pendleton

Takes map from its snap holder
Extreme edge of instrument panel

Grabs a ruler

Begins calculation
The speed of the objects

Calculate and flying
At the same time

Calculate and flying

Lands at Pendleton

Large airfield

A group of people

Wait to greet him

No one is saying anything

Just looking at him

They know something happened

Somebody phoned them
From Yakima

Some of them are local press

A tremendously bright flash

Pulsating

Pulsating

Puffs a Chesterfield

Listen to his story

Listen

A bunch of them
Help him finish his calculation

FORMATION

How fast they flew
39.9 miles

Conservative estimate:
1350 miles per hour

Probably faster

Faster

Must be guided missiles

Military always working on something

Robotically controlled

1350 miles per hour

The human body
Cannot withstand

The flipping, erratic movement
Of these strange craft

Cannot withstand

One of the craft

Looked different
From the rest

Different shape

Like a crescent

A crescent

A tremendously bright flash

Pulsating

Like a jelly fish

Tells reporters

They wobbled and flipped

Like saucers
Skipping on the water

They don't have a name
Until today

A flying saucer

The name catches on

No one is sure
Who said it first

Tremendously bright flash

So brilliant

Lights up whole cockpit

**Arnold has the makings
Of a reliable witness**

**He is a respected businessman
And pilot**

**Seems to neither
Be exaggerating**

What he sees

**Or adding sensational details
To his report**

Doesn't have moment's peace

FORMATION

Not a moment's peace

Flying saucers

They don't have a names

They are here

They are here

Tremendously bright flash

They number nine

Flying diagonally

Echelon formation

A preacher calls him

Tells him the objects
He saw are

Harbingers of doomsday

Preparing my congregation

For the end of the world

A woman in a Pendleton Café

Notices him on the street

Dashes out shrieking

There's the man
Who saw the men from Mars

Sobs

I have to do something
For the children

I have to do something!

> *Tremendously bright flash*
>
> *So brilliant*
>
> *Lights up whole cockpit*

A fisherman's report

Of seeing purplish spheres

With portholes

Flutter and sail

Maneuver over the Crown River

Flutter and sail

In Ontario

Are not meteors

Nor are they fragments

Of a comet

Or Venus

Prospector named Fred Johnson

On Mount Adams

Says he saw six objects

On June 24h

FORMATION

At about the same time
As Arnold

Viewed through small telescope

Round

Tapered sharply
To a point in the head

And in an oval shape

Reports to Army Air Force Intelligence

The end of the world

Portland Oregon Journal

Receives letter
From L.G. Bernier
Richland, Washington

Was 110 miles east
Of Mount Adams

And 140 miles southeast
Of Mount Rainer

Saw three
Of the strange objects

Almost edgewise

Toward Mount Rainer

About one half hour
Before Arnold

Thought they
Part of a larger formation

I have seen a P-38 appear

Seemingly on one horizon

And then be gone to the opposite horizon

In no time at all

But these discs

Were certainly traveling faster
Than any P-38

60 miles west–northwest
Of Richmond

Yakima, Washington

Woman named
Ethel Wheelhouse

Reports several flying discs

Moving at fantastic speed

At around the same time
As Arnold's sighting

A member of the
Washington State Forest Service

Fire watch at a tower
In Diamond Gap

20 miles south of Yakima

Reports seeing flashes
At 3 pm

FORMATION

On the 24th
Over Mount Rainer

Exactly at the same time
As Arnold's sighting

A pilot of DC-4

Some ten to fifteen miles
North of Arnold

En route to Seattle

Reports seeing nothing unusual

Same DC-4
That Arnold saw

What are these saucers?

These flying saucers

When Arnold goes home

Receives 10,000 pieces of mail

10,000

He is the most famous man
In the world

Most famous man
In the world

This whole thing
Has gotten out of hand

I want to talk to the FBI
Or someone

Half the people
Think I'm some sort of combination

Of Einstein, Flash Gordon
And a screwball

10,000 letters

There is a lot of foolishness
Going on

A lot of foolishness

But he keeps watching the news wires

A letter from editor Ray Palmer
Venture Press, Evanston, Illinois

Science fiction magazine?

Not the kind of stuff I read

Wants him to recount experience
For one of his magazines

Sends Palmer report
He sent to AAF Intelligence

Palmer writes back

2 harbor patrolmen
Tacoma, Washington

Had a very unusual experience

Place called Maury Island

These fellows Harold Dahl
And Fred Crisman

FORMATION

Claim they have not only
Seen a group of flying saucers

But have in their possession
Some fragments

That came from one of them

Fragments

Swear they're not lying

Blue-white flashes emit
From the center

Of their surfaces

Pulsating

Pulsating

Mr. Palmer has definite
Interest in their story

Fragments

Blue white flashes

Like jelly fish

Would like to send
Him expense money

And investigate
Authenticity of the story

As well as ship
Some of the fragments

If you obtain them

Would you consider my proposal
Mr. Arnold?

Would you consider my proposal?

Fragments

Tremendously bright flash

Now they have a name

His wife Doris

The phone doesn't stop ringing Ken
It doesn't stop ringing

I'm sorry honey

Letters

Telegrams

Phone calls

Reporters

Press agencies

All over the world

I'm the only sane one of the bunch

Other sightings?

Keeps careful track of them

Won't be long
Before one of these things
Is in every garage

FORMATION

Dave Johnson
Aviation Editor
Idaho Statesman

Doubts his story

Because he is in position
To know

Not a military guided missile

If what you've seen
Is true

It did not belong
To the good ol' USA

Would you consider my proposal,
Mr. Arnold?

Blue-white flashes emit
From the center

Of the surfaces

His friend
Colonel Paul Wieland

Just returned from Germany

Served on Malmedy Case

And on Nuremburg Trials
As a judge

Phones him

Ken, let's go fishing

Now that's the best idea
I've heard in days

Get their tackles together

Leave their wives
To guard the fort

His wife Doris

Don't forget Kiska
In Swan Lake

That's not for weeks honey
I'll just be gone a few days

I know but don't get too distracted
I know you Ken

I won't miss Kiska
Don't worry

Princess Odette

The Swan Queen

Heroine of the story

Transferred into a swan

Lives by lake

Magically transformed
From the tears

Of her grieving mother

After Von Rothbart kidnapped her

The Swan Queen

FORMATION

Practices by piano

Tutu leotard
White pink

Glitter

Bedroom ballerina

Straight legs
Pointed feet

Plies, pirouettes.
Poise

Floor formations

Take off in his plane

Sekiu, Washington

Way out on the
Olympic Peninsula

Fishing should be
At its best

And a long way
From people

Beautiful, calm flight

Land in a cow pasture

All during flight
Keeps newly purchased
Movie camera ready

Just in case

Just in case

They number nine

Flying diagonally

Echelon formation

Chinook

Sekiu King Salmon

Blue, green, red
Or purple on the back
And top of the heads

Silvery sides

White ventral surfaces

Black spots
On its tail

Upper half of body

Let's get a 40 incher
Size of a freighter!

Rich red meat
Translucent and buttery

If your lure is
Putting out erratic vibrations

20 to 30 feet

From school of chinooks

You can pull him in

Like a magnet

FORMATION

Follow the vibration

Like a radar beam

Attack your bait

Likes rough water

Depend on each other

We just find the baitfish

We'll find the salmon

Rancher of the pasture

Lets them keep the plane there

Drives them down

To village
By ocean inlet

All set for some
Really good fishing

But the fisherman
Are not in their boats

They have not even gone fishing

The water red

Red as blood

Thousands of chinook
Have died

A man died
From eating oysters

Red jelly-like substance
Everywhere

High concentration
Of karenia brevis blooms

Blooms

Density
Tens of millions of cells

Per liter of seawater

Dead fish
Float everywhere

Silver
Glinting in the sun

Next morning

Take short boat ride

Around the inlet

Even if the fish
Are worth eating

Can't be caught

Leaping
Out of the water

As high as six feet

Leaping

Skipping across the water

FORMATION

Trying to shake off
Jelly-like substance

Poisoning them

Nothing to do
But turn around

And fly home

Leave the cow pasture

Circle high
Over village of Sekiu

Can see the red water

The bloom

Pulsating

It looks like

It has fallen out of the sky

Fallen out of the sky

When he gets back

Sees the news stories

Purchases every newspaper

At Terminal Building newsstand

The crew of a United Airlines flight

Have seen the discs too

The flying saucers

For 15 minutes

15 minutes

He has to find them

Talk to them

Blue white flashes emit
From the center

Of their surfaces

Fragments

The bloom

Falling out of the sky

★★

I swear I'm not lying
I swear it

Fragments

Hot, almost molten

Raining down

From the doughnut-shaped craft

Seaman Harold Dahl

And the others

Run for shelter

Under a cliff
On the beach

FORMATION

Behind logs

One of the falling fragments

Hits and kills Chip
Their dog

Yelps

Yelps

Chip!

No!!

Chip!

Rain of metal

What are they?

What are they?

The strange aircraft

Lift slowly

Drift westward

Out to sea

Light shines on them

Through the clouds

They are brilliant

Not one brilliance

But of many brilliances

Like the dashboard
Of a brand new Buick

Lift

Disappear

At tremendous height

The center aircraft

That had spewed debris

Not hindered
In its flight

Remains in center

Of formation

All rise

And disappear

Out to sea

What the hell just happened?

Try to pick up
Several pieces

Of the metal

Too hot

Scorching

All rise

And disappear

FORMATION

After some cool off

They load considerable number

Aboard the boat

Touch the metal

That looked
Like falling newspaper

What just happened?

His son's arm injured

Sobbing about Chip

We'll bury him at sea son

We'll bury him at sea

Confetti

Or thousands
Of newspapers

From somewhere
Inside the center

Please tell me
What just happened?

They discuss
What they saw for a while

Dahl attempts
To radio from the North Queen

Nothing

Static so great

Impossible to reach radio station

Impossible

That's a good radio too

Must be those things

Wheelhouse on boat
Hit and damaged

By the falling debris

Not one brilliance

But of many brilliances

Many brilliances

Start the engine

Go directly to Tacoma

First aid for his boy
At the hospital

When reaches dock

Tells his superior office

Fred L. Crisman

Short, stout man

Very serious about the work

Tells him

Gives him a look

FORMATION

What the fuck did you do to the boat, Dahl?
Who's going to pay for this?
Who?

Tells him

Tells him whole story

You drinking Dahl?
You expect me to buy this shit?

I swear I'm not lying
I swear it

Go out there

Look for yourself Fred

They were round

Completely round

But appeared a little squashed
On top and bottom

Like someone placed
A large board
On an inner tube

And squashed it

I'm scared Fred

Gives him the film
From the camera

Get it developed

Please get it developed

I will
And I'll go out there
And take a look around

There's debris Fred

Fragments

Confetti

Thousands of newspapers

Not one brilliance

But of many brilliances

Many brilliances

All rise

And disappear

The next morning
7 am

Harold's doorbell rings

A gentleman
In a black suit

Fedora hat
Medium height

About 40 years of age

Smiles
Corner of his mouth

FORMATION

I would like to take you to breakfast
I have something to discuss with you

Not particularly unusual

Probably a lumber buyer

Buying salvaged logs

Frequently call on him
Early in the morning

Looks like an insurance salesman

But accepts his invitation

Walk out to the curb

Sees the man's automobile
Shiny, black 1947 Buick Roadmaster

The gentleman suggests
Dahl drive his own car

And follow him

Smiles
Corner of his mouth

While driving downtown
Tries to get a look

At the license plate number
On the car

He is following

But doesn't see a plate

All rise

And disappear

Just buying some salvaged logs

That's all

Not one brilliance

But of many brilliances

Maybe he wants to buy
Some equipment from me

No license plate

Does seem odd

That this man
Is taking Harold for breakfast

In uptown section
Of Tacoma

Rather than lower dock section

Which is usual place

Where loggers
And salvaging operators congregate

Stop in front of
Sally's Silver Spoon Café

They go inside

Seated in a booth
By the window

Look at their menus

FORMATION

Harold just wants to ask him
Why they're here

But doesn't

Orders steak and eggs
And coffee

Man smiles
Corner of his mouth

Orders 3 glazed donuts
And tea

Lights a Winston
Starts to talk

Blows a ring

Begins to tell Harold
With great accuracy

Everything

Everything

Entire trip yesterday

The six objects

The fragments

Dead dog

Damaged boat

Smiles
Corner of his mouth

Blows another ring

How do you know this?

Who told you?

Smiles
A chipped tooth

Swallows some donut

What I have said
Is proof that I know

A great deal more

About this experience of yours

Then you will ever want to believe

You should not have seen what you saw

If you love your family

And don't want anything to happen

To their general welfare

You will not discuss this experience of yours

With anyone

With anyone

Do you hear me?

Smiles
Corner of his mouth

Blows another ring

Through the clouds

FORMATION

They are brilliant

Not one brilliance

But of many brilliances

Do you hear me?

All rise

And disappear

★★

They are here

They have been here a long time

And now they have a name

> *Tremendously bright flash*
>
> *So brilliant*
>
> *Lights up whole cockpit*

Kenneth Arnold

Buys up all of the newspapers

Terminal Building newsstand

In one of the papers

The Seattle Times

There is even a photograph

The first photograph

Of a flying saucer

That he has ever seen

His hands are shaking

Shaking

Lights a Chesterfield

Puffs

Puffs

Of a disc

A flying disc

They have been here a long time

A long time

Photo taken
By fellow named Frank Ryman

Coast Guard yeoman

Taken the night before

Rushes madly uptown

I have to see a blow up
Of this picture

To Seattle office

International Press Service

They number nine

Flying diagonally

Echelon formation

FORMATION

Fragments

Blue whites flashes

Pulsating

Pulsating

A blow up of the picture

Rushes in

So many hills in Seattle

Completely out of breath

Finds a reporter

Can I see a blow up
Of that flying disc?

Slow down fella
Who are you?

He's reporter shy
By now

It will be a circus
If he tells him

But has no choice

I'm Kenneth Arnold

The Kenneth Arnold?

Grabs him by the arm

Rushes him from his office

Down the anteroom
Of the news building

Enter a conference room

I think you folks need to meet

Sitting at a table

Captain EJ Smith

And his co-pilot Ralph Stevens

Of the United Airlines DC-3 crew

That saw them too

Holy Cow!

Gazing at a blow up
Of the photograph

Taken by Frank Wyman

Arnold shakes their hands

What a big guy
This Smith fellow is

Feels like he is
Shaking hands

With the big transport he flies

Big toothy grin

They all examine the photograph

Yep, that's what we saw

FORMATION

They all go out
For coffee and talk

The flipping, erratic movement
Of these strange craft

Flutter and sail

One of the craft

Looked different
From the rest

Darker

Different shape

Like a crescent

A tremendously bright flash

Pulsating

Like a jellyfish

Pulsating

Fallen out of the sky

Smith and his co-pilot
Tell Arnold their story

Smith does most of the talking

Landed in Boise, Idaho

Shortly before 9 last night

July 4th

Afraid they were late
In their schedule

Took off promptly
9:04

Weather perfect

Right before take off

He was climbing aboard
DC-3

Someone in the cabin
Asked if he had seen

Any of these flying saucers

No, of course not

Not only had he never seen one

He didn't believe
There were such things

But replies

I'll believe them
When I see one

7,000 feet over
Emmett, Idaho

Saw not just one
But nine of them

Nine of them

Thought it was group
Of light planes

FORMATION

Returning from
July 4th celebration

Nine of them

Not aircraft they knew

Flat and circular

First group of five

Appeared to open
And close

In formation

Then veered
To the left

Picks up
Radio microphone

Ontario, Oregon C.A.A
Radio Communications Station

45 miles northwest

Didn't tell them
What he was seeing

Step outside
And look to the northwest
About 15 miles
And tell me what you see

He sees nothing

Nothing

First group of discs
Disappears

Another group of three
Appears

And a fourth disc
Off by itself

Transport at 8,000 feet altitude

Cruising

Over rugged country

Leading to Blue Mountain

Towards Pendleton, Oregon

His co-pilot and he
See exactly the same thing

Objects seemed to merge
And disappear

Then come back in sight

And vanish again
In northwest

It is not fireworks

Reflections

Or smoke

Not aircraft
They are familiar with

FORMATION

I don't know how fast
They were going

But we all saw them

We saw them

Flat on the bottom

Circular

And seem rough on top

Bigger than their aircraft

It's just amazing
Simply amazing

Their stewardess

Saw them too

She saw them

A tremendously bright flash

So brilliant

Pulsating

Pulsating

Lights up whole cockpit

Fragments

Blue-white flashes emit
From the center

It did not belong
To the good ol' USA

MATT BIALER

Chinook jumping

Skipping on water

Leaping

The red bloom

Fallen out of the sky

Fallen out of the sky

Arnold visited by
Two representatives

Of A-2 Military Intelligence
Of the Fourth Air Force

Lieutenant Frank M. Brown
Captain William Davidson

Happy to see them

Can't understand
Why it's taken days

For them to reach out
To him

Arnold and wife Doris
Impressed by their kindness

And consideration
Of the peculiar position

Flying saucers
Have put him in

Meet at Hotel Owyhee
In Boise

FORMATION

Treat him and Doris
To wonderful dinner

Candlelight
Filet mignon
Chappellet Cabernet Sauvignon

Jovial but serious

Their faces light up

Brown
Tall and handsome
Easy going southern drawl

Davidson
Short, stocky fellow

Medium complexion

When he smiles
Notice long scar on his face

Discuss various phases
Of his observation

Frankly we don't know
What you saw

We don't know what they are

It's not us

They are going
To talk to Captain Smith too

After dinner
He invited Davidson and Brown

Back to the house

Talk under better circumstances

They each escort Doris
Up the front walk

Their two girls
Have been put to bed

Have the house
To themselves

Ask him
A lot of questions

They take notes

Draws picture for them

His speed calculation

Can we keep this stuff?

Of course you can

Doesn't know why
But doesn't tell them

That one of the discs
In formation

Looked different

Darker

The crescent

Maybe it was just
The angle he saw it from

FORMATION

The crescent

Not positive it was one

Hasn't even told Doris

Return them to their hotel

Each kiss Doris' hand

Ken, call us if anything
Of unusual nature
Comes to your attention
Or if you need help in any way

Call us collect

At A-2 Fourth Air Force

Hamilton Field, California

Call us collect

And let's keep quiet

About this

Better for all concerned

Better for all concerned

They're polite,
Considerate

He trusts them

Trusts them

Another letter
From Ray Palmer

Editor
Venture Press

Fly to Tacoma

Investigate the sighting

And the fragments

Meet those Dahl
And Crisman fellows

Honey, I'm going to
Accept Ray Palmer's offer

I can't not accept

I'm just too curious

I need answers

I know you do Ken
I hope you find them

Don't forget Kiska

Swan Lake

You can't be gone for weeks

I know

Don't buy another horse
While I'm gone

We already have a menagerie

Horses
Cows
Pigs

FORMATION

Writes to Palmer

Requests $200 expense money
Hotel and food

$200 at Western Union
The next morning

He's going to Tacoma

Princess Odette

The Swan Queen

Transformed into a swan

Lives by a lake

Magically transformed

From the tears
Of her grieving mother

The only way
For the spell to be broken

The power of eternal love

Between Odette
And young man

Who remains faithful
To her

For if the vow
Of eternal love

Is broken

She will remain
A swan forever

A swan forever

They dance

And leap

They number nine

Flying diagonally

Echelon formation

Blue-white flashes emit
From the center

Of their surfaces

Similar in pulsation
And rhythm and beating

Of the human heart

★★

Dusk

Kenneth Arnold
Lands at Barry's Airport

Little airfield
Located down on the mud flats

Outside Tacoma

Neither Barry
Nor his wife recognize him

FORMATION

As the man
Whose face

Has been all over the newspapers

All over the newspapers

Most famous man in the world

Flying Saucer Man

Barry gasses up his plane

Ties it up for the night

Arnold starts calling
All of the hotels in town

Can't find a room

I should have called ahead

Barry's wife keeps saying

Getting a room in Tacoma

Very difficult

Severe housing shortage

Keeps calling

Hotels

Motels

Rooming houses

All over the newspapers

Most famous man in the world

Flying Saucer Man

On a lark
Calls the Winthrop Hotel

Largest and most prominent hotel
In all of Tacoma

Oh I am sure they're booked
They're the Winthrop

Room clerk

Yes Mr. Arnold
We have a room and a bath for you

There already was
A reservation in his name

There already was

Who could've done that?

He didn't

And neither did Palmer

Are you sure
You have a room for Kenneth Arnold?

Clerk goes back
To check cards and papers

Yes Sir. We have a room
Reserved for you Mr. Arnold

How can that be?

The clerk doesn't know more

FORMATION

I have never stayed there before

Must be another Kenneth Arnold

But he's desperate for a room

And he'll deal
With that later

If this other Arnold shows up

Maybe he'd share it

Two Kenneth Arnolds
In a room

I'll be right over

A tremendously bright flash

So brilliant

Pulsating

Pulsating

Like a jellyfish

Lights up whole cockpit

Fragments

Blue–white flashes emit
From the center

It does not belong
To the good ol' USA

While in Tacoma

Wants to keep low profile

*If the newspapers
Find out I'm here*

They'll be running me ragged

He doesn't want that

Most famous man in the world

All over the newspapers

Flying Saucer Man

It is already
Too out of hand

Too out of hand

Don't forget Kiska

Odette

The Swan Queen

If the vow
Of eternal love is broken

She will remain a swan forever

A swan forever

Falls in love

With Prince Siegfried

Arrives at lakeside clearing

Just as flock of swans

Land nearby

FORMATION

Aims his crossbow

When one of them

Turns into a beautiful maiden

Beautiful Maiden

Plie and releve

Bend and rise

Plie and releve

They number nine

Flying diagonally

Echelon formation

Arrives at hotel

Signs the register

Grabs the key

Hears of upcoming strike

Workers in the hotel

No elevators
If it happens

Fabulous

Room 502

Twin beds

And a bath

Tired but grabs
Phone book

Looks for
One Harold A. Dahl

Several Dahls

Phones H. A. Dahl

Finds he is the fellow
He came to see

Tells him who he is

Flying Saucer Man

I know who you are
Everybody does
I'm not going to talk to you Mr. Arnold
Go back home

Forget the whole business

And why is that Mr. Dahl?
Why won't you talk to me?

I will not talk about
Or discuss the matter
Of these flying discs
With anyone

With anyone

Keeps him on the phone

I came all the way
From Boise

FORMATION

I of all people
Am sympathetic

To your feelings

I of all people

Doggone it
I can't leave without an audience

Please

Nothing but tough luck
Ever since whole business started
Nothing but tough luck
Better off if we left the subject alone

But out of respect

For the long way you came

I will come to the hotel

To meet you within half hour

Flying Saucer Man

He's tired

Hoping he'd meet Dahl
Next day

But this might be
Only chance

Only chance

And he's curious
Who he is

And these fragments

Fragments

Like speed boats
On rough water

The tail of a Chinese kite
Blowing in the wind

Like a saucer

If you skipped it
Across the water

Like a saucer

Yes, please come

Half hour later
A rap on his door

Surprised that such
A frightened person

Is as big a guy
As Dahl

Over six foot two inches

Well over 200 pounds

A two fisted lumberjack

Invited him in

Moves to large chair
From near the dresser

In between the two beds

FORMATION

Arnold talks

Throwing in some questions
For Dahl

Wait a minute Mr. Arnold
Not so fast
If I talk
There are a number of things
I want you to consider
If you want me
To tell you my story

In fact I think I better go home

Stay a while

Have a smoke

Offers him a Chesterfield

Mr. Arnold
I still think it
Would be good advice to you
This flying saucer business
Is the most complicated thing
You ever got mixed up in

Trust me

I know

Next two hours
Dahl tells Arnold

His story

21st of June

Two hours

Nearly lost his job
His wife

He's been sick

Lost a tremendously
Boom of logs

That he had salvaged

From the bay

When an unusual tide

Somehow broke the moorings
One night

Unusual tide

Lost $3500

His boat still
Half broken

Puffing on the smoke

Everyone has a tough time
Harold

Doesn't mean the sighting
Has anything to do with it

The sighting

Tells him the whole story

Whole story

FORMATION

I swear I'm not lying
I swear it

Their donut shapes

They make no sound

No sound

One hundred feet
In diameter

Each has a hole
In the center

25 feet in diameter

Shell-like
Gold silver

Their surfaces
Seem of metal

Metal

Appear to be burled

When light
Shines in them

Through the clouds

They are brilliant

Not one brilliance

But of many brilliances

Many brilliances

I swear I'm not lying
I swear it

Tells the whole story

Center one
Almost crashes

Almost crashes

Begins spewing forth

What seems like

Confetti

Or thousands
Of newspapers

Tells the whole story

Another smoke

Gets up from
Where he is sitting

Edge of bed

Paces

Let me take you
Out to my secretary's house
A few of the fragments
I brought back are there

Fragments

Hitting the beach

Fragments

FORMATION

An unusual tide

Dead fish
Float everywhere

Silver
Glinting in the sun

Can see the red water

The bloom

Pulsating

It looks like

It has fallen out of the sky

Fallen out of the sky

Leave hotel

Drive in Harold's car

Out to his secretary's house

Plain little house
Stands all alone on corner

Evening bright
And clear

Ten minutes to get there

Walks up
Cracked sidewalk

To wooden porch
With no screens

White spindle-like porch supports

Place could use a paint job

Harold knocks
On side of doorway

Opens screen door

Enough light to see

House of about 1910 vintage

Turns doorknob
On the main door

Oblong little
Grape insignia

Door of dark mahogany

Stained glass window
On door

Green and red

Of an orchid

Oak floor inside

A piano
To the left

Steinway

Like ours

Against the wall

A piano

Kiska

FORMATION

She will remain a swan forever

A swan forever

He aims his crossbow

At the swans

But freezes

When one of them

Turns into a beautiful maiden

Odette at first

Terrified of Siegfried

Promises not to harm her

Promises not to harm her

A swan forever

Plie, releve

And saute

Bend, rise

And leap

Leap

Next to the piano

By west window

A large radio

1937 model
Walnut cabinet

Wires trailing

Through the edge of the window

Panel to the outside

Can see
From reflected light

Of the room

The aerial going up

Outside the house

Base of the aerial
Two 2 x 25

Follows Harold
Through the first room

Dining room

And into the kitchen
Painted green

A woman of 40 years
Of age

Blond
His secretary

Smoking

Deeply engrossed

Writing checks

Dock work

FORMATION

Papers, receipts
Notes

Laid out
Every available space

Jeanie this is Kenneth Arnold
The man in the news

He brings Arnold
Back to front room

Tells him to sit down

And wait a moment

Be right back

Sits on edge
Of piano bench

Comes back

Hands Arnold

A dark colored
Rock ash tray

Here is one of the fragments
We've been using it as an ashtray

Arnold chuckles

I hate to break this to you Harold
But that's only a piece of lava rock

Like from a volcano

Harold shakes his head

Waves him off

I don't know much about metal Mr. Arnold
But that's some of the stuff
That hit our boat

There's twenty tons of it out there

Doesn't have any
Of the white metal

But Fred Crisman
Has whole box full

In his garage

They are here

They have always been here

They number nine

Flying diagonally

Echelon formation

A tremendously bright flash

Lights up his whole cockpit

Whole cockpit

Next morning

Banging on his hotel door

9:30 am

Both Crisman and Dahl

FORMATION

Crisman
Short, stocky fellow

Dark complexioned

Very alert
Full of energy

Not afraid
Like Dahl

Shakes Arnold's hand

Practically bubbles over

To tell his story

Thought Dahl
Had been drinking

Cussing him out
About damaging boat

But how could
Poor navigation

Account for the damage?

Went out to the island

Went out to the island

Stood on the shore
Looking for fragments

Some kind of aircraft

Came out of cumulous cloud

Some kind of aircraft

Donut shaped
With portholes

Wide circle over the bay

Couldn't believe what he was seeing

Dahl was right

Dahl was right

No visible means of propulsion

Large inner tube
With round eyes or portholes

No sound

Circled the bay

As if looking for something

Looking for something

**I hold a commercial
Pilot's license**

**I flew over 100 missions
In fighter aircraft**

Over Burma

I feel qualified

**To describe it
Accurately**

I feel qualified

Appeared to be metal

FORMATION

Burled and of brassy color

Almost golden

As the sun hit it

Showed more brilliance

Than a solid polished
Surface would show

Arnold confused

Doesn't know what to think

Was that ashtray metal?

I'm not qualified to investigate this

I'm no Perry Mason

I'm no Perry Mason

He asks to see photographs
That Dahl took

And the white metal
Stored in Crisman's garage

Gets another idea

Smithy!

Will call the United Airlines pilot

To help him
Get to the bottom of this

Captain EJ Smith

Big Smithy

Do you guys mind
If I invite someone to help me investigate this?

He'll come
I know he will

Smithy!

A tremendously bright flash

Lights up whole cockpit

Like a welder's arc light

A welder's arc light

★★

Kenneth Arnold
Able to reach EJ Smith
On the phone

Smithy

Has afternoon off

Would like to join
In the investigation

Arnold will fly
Up to Seattle right away

Meet him
In front of Terminal Building

Fly him back
To Tacoma

FORMATION

He would like Smithy's company

Feels he is
More qualified

To judge Dahl's
And Crisman's stories

Than he is

By the time
Arnold gets there

Smithy is waiting
For him

Quick cup of coffee

Updates him
About Tacoma

Maury Island

How puzzled he is

Smithy's enthusiastic
About coming

Let's go

Climb into
Arnold's plane

The look
On Smithy's face

When they take off

He's been flying
DC-3s from Seattle
To Chicago

You sure this thing can fly Ken?
This thing made of cardboard?

Funny looking
One engine plane

One of the only things
That is metal

Is the engine

Mountain plane Smithy!

Smithy chuckles
At the airspeed

105 miles per hour

Arnold has his
Movie camera ready
Just in case

Just in case

A tremendously bright flash

Lights up whole cockpit

Whole cockpit

Pulsating

Like a jellyfish

Pulsating

FORMATION

Fallen out of the sky

Arrive in Tacoma
About 3 pm

Park airplane
Barry's Airport

Fred Crisman waiting

Drives them to hotel

Would then go back

Pick up Dah;

Be around an hour

Arnold tells them
No newspaper reporters

No publicity

About what
They're doing here

And United Airlines
Doesn't need to know

Flying Saucer Man

Go directly
To the room

502

Phone down
To order

Coffee and rolls

And a pack
Of Chesterfields

An hour and a half later

Dahl and Crisman arrive

Smithy:

I'm going to stay
Until I find out what gives
We're going to get to the bottom of this boys

Starts cross examination
Of Dahl and Crisman

Every possible phase
Of everybody's relationships

And experiences
Up to the present

Six very large

Doughnut shaped aircraft

2000 feet up
Above the water

Almost directly overhead

Are those balloons?

What are they?

What are they?

I swear I'm not lying
I swear it

FORMATION

The one in the
Center of the formation

Stationary
But wobbling

No motors

Propellers

Any visible signs
Of propulsion

They make no sound

No sound

When light
Shines on them

Through the clouds

They are brilliant

Not one brilliance

But of many brilliances

Many brilliances

Center aircraft

Begins spewing forth

What seems like

Confetti

Or thousands
Of newspapers

Confetti

Flutters to earth

Flutters to earth

All rise

And disappear

The gentleman
In the black suit

Fedora hat
Medium height

About 40 years of age

Shiny black 1947 Buick Roadster

Smiles
Corner of this mouth

Smoke rings

You should not have seen what you saw
You will not discuss this experience
With anyone

With anyone

Do you hear me?

Smithy wants to
Stay extra days

Goes back to Seattle
To get automobile
And toothbrush

FORMATION

Phones United Airlines

Cancels his flights
Next few days

He is visiting a sick friend

A sick friend

Comes back to Tacoma

He and Arnold

Drive somewhere for supper

Anywhere

Let's just drive

Light green Deluxe
Model Town and Country Chrysler

Back at 10 pm

Smithy walks over
Flops on Arnold's bed

Knocks pillow down

Reveals .32 automatic pistol

A little nervous Ken?

I don't know why
I brought it along

I don't know why

Conversation drifts
From the fragments

To red tides

Seiku King Salmon

Chinook

Blue, green, red
Or purple on the back
And top of heads

Silvery sides

White ventral surfaces

The water red

Red as blood

Thousands of Chinook
Have died

Red jelly-like substance
Everywhere

Blooms

Density
Tens of millions of cells

Per liter of seawater

Dead fish
Float everywhere

Silver
Glinting in the sun

The bloom

Pulsating

FORMATION

It looks like

It has fallen out of the sky

Fallen out of the sky

Fish leaping

Skipping across the water

Don't forget Kiska
Swan Lake

Princess Odette

The Swan Queen

Kiska
Leaping with Siegfried

He was tricked
By Von Rothbart

He broke the vow

She will remain
A swan forever

A swan forever

The crashed C-40 Marine transport plane

Has finally been found

Southwest side
Of Mount Rainer

32 men aboard

In severe distress

Badly off course

Freezing fog

Pounding sleet

The plane
And 32 souls aboard

Has vanished

Vanished

Help us

Help us find our boys

Find the plane

You will be rewarded

$5000

Fulfillment of a dream

George Stoker of Richland
120 miles from Mount Adams

Says he saw
A strange glow

A strange glow

Has finally been found

Family must be relieved

But they can't get
To the bodies

Top of the mountain

FORMATION

Conditions too treacherous

Fulfillment of a dream

Is this all a hoax?

Are Dahl and Crisman lying?

What reason
Would they have?

What reason?

Maybe it's the Russians

Baiting us

On the whole affair

Very simple reason:

To find out
What we actually know

About these flying saucers

These flying saucers

What we know

Flying Saucer Man

They number nine

Flying diagonally

Echelon formation

Start to doze off

Phone rings

Ted Morello

Of United Press

UP's head man
In Tacoma

Offices in
Tacoma Times Building

Arnold immediately
Starts to hang up

Wait! Don't hang up Arnold!
Hold on a minute
Some crackpot has been
Phoning me here
Telling us verbatim
What has been going on
In your hotel room

*I will not admit
Or deny anything*

Tells Arnold
Step by step

What they have
Been doing all day

Step by step

What they have been saying
Discussing

Everything

Arnold amazed by the accuracy

FORMATION

Stunned

But doesn't let on
That it's all true

Stunned

Hands phone
To Smithy

Listens

Nods

Hangs up

It's either our friends Crisman and Dahl
Or we're being bugged

Search the place

Search for hidden wire

A Dictaphone

Tear the room apart

Search the place

Mattresses

Under cushions

Cabinets

The phone itself

Picture frames

Tear the room apart

Search the place

Behind the mirror

But they find nothing

Nothing

Tremendously bright flash

So brilliant

Lights up whole cockpit

Whole cockpit

Flutter and sail

Tip their wings

One of the craft

Looked different
From the rest

Darker

Different shape

Like a crescent

A crescent

Next morning
Crisman and Dahl arrive

Arms loaded
With heavy lava rock fragments

And Crisman has brought
A number of pieces

FORMATION

Of the white metal

White metal

That he says
Came from the center aircraft

Inspect every fragment
Dark lava-like substance

Perfectly smooth
On one side

Slightly curved

While other side
Looks like it has

Been subjected
To intense heat

Heavy and brass colored

Even the smaller pieces
Quite a labor to lift

Lining to some sort
Of power tube?

Hands them piece
Of the white metal

Very light

Almost seems
Like aluminum

Which certain sections
Of all large aircraft made of

If this is the white stuff
That Dahl claims

Came out of the craft

Then it has to be a fake

It has to be a fake

Seen hundreds of piles
Of them in salvage dumps

One unusual thing
Makes them wonder

Makes them wonder

One piece
Can plainly see

That two parts of it
Have been riveted

Rivets not round
But square

Never seen
That type of rivet

Crisman must know

Being a pilot himself

That they would recognize
The white metal

Can you show us the photos?

Crisman describes them

FORMATION

They were not good shots

Spots on them

Unable to locate

Sure he has them
In office down at the dock

Will try to find them

Sure he has them

I swear I'm not lying
I swear it

Chip is barking

Five of the strange aircraft

Circle

Very slowly

Around sixth one

Stationary but wobbly

Falling rapidly

Around sixth one

Some sort of trouble

Some sort of trouble

Why would they be lying?

Why?

Let's call Military Intelligence

I know these two fellows

Army Air Force

Brown and Davidson

They're good men

They'll get to the bottom of this

Smith:
It might be a good idea

Crisman nods

Very enthusiastic
About meeting Military Intelligence

Dahl
Frightened

Shakes his head

No, I'm done with all of this
If you call them
I won't talk to them
My story is true
Fred Crisman knows it
He can tell it for me

Later
Arnold calls his wife Doris

I have to stay a few more days

I have to

I can't let this go

FORMATION

Ok, just be back
For Kisko's recital

I will
I will

Or I might buy another horse

Ok, I promise it won't be long

Practices by piano

Tutu leotard
White pink

Bedroom ballerina

Straight legs
Pointed toes

Plies, pirouettes
Poise

Floor formations

The Swan Queen

Will remain
A swan forever

Odette at first
Terrified of Siegfried

Promises not to harm her

Tells him
She is the Swan Queen Odette

She and her friends
Victims of a terrible spell

A terrible spell

Cast by the evil
Owl-like sorcerer Von Rothbart

Turned into swans

Only at night

By the side of the enchanted lake

Created from the tears
Of Odette's grieving mother

The spell can be broken

If one who has never loved before

Swears to love Odette forever

Swears

Love Odette forever

They dance

Saute

Leap

Glitter
Flutters down

Glitter

A terrible spell

Remain a swan forever

★★

FORMATION

They don't have a name
Until now

When he has the sighting

They are here

They have been here a long time

And now they have a name

Kenneth Arnold

Flying Saucer Man

They number nine

Flying diagonally

Echelon formation

Picks up the telephone

Calls collect

As Lt. Brown
Insisted he should

A-2 Military Intelligence

Fourth Air Force

Hamilton Field, California

Calls specifically
Person to person

Lt. Frank M. Brown

Gives his name
To operator

So Brown would know
Who is calling him

They don't have a name
Until now

When he has the sighting

They are here

Know
Who is calling him

Hears vaguely
The conversation

At the other end
Of the line

Lt. Brown refuses
To take the collect call

On the military line

Tells the operator
To notify Mr. Arnold

That he will
Call him back

Immediately
From base pay phone

Why wouldn't he
Talk to him

On the military line?

FORMATION

Impression that not only
Is Lt. Brown a brilliant fellow

But takes
All possible precautions

All possible precautions

Lt. Brown
Calls back

Arnold
Recognizes his voice

Slow, easy
Southern drawl

Tells Brown
Everything that is going on

He and Smithy

The harbor patrolmen

Maury Island

The doughnut-shaped craft

The fragments

Brown:

Sit tight
If we don't call you back
Within an hour
We'll be there

We'll be there

The telephone rings again

Paul Lance
Tacma Times

Can I talk to you guys?
Can I –

Arnold hangs up

Rings again

Sigh

Picks it up

Ted Morello
Of UP

Says that
This crackpot character

Been phoning him
From pay telephone

Limits his conversation
15 to 20 seconds

Says voice
That has been calling him

So frequently last 2 days

Often while
Crisman and Dahl

Are in the room
So it can't be them

Guy tells them
Everything

FORMATION

Everything

Trying to figure out
Who character is

Who is he?

They don't have a name
Until now

When he has the sighting

Tremendously bright flash

So brilliant

Pulsating

Pulsating

Lights up whole cockpit

Whole cockpit

Like a welder's arc light

Fragments

Blue-white flashes emit
From the center

It did not belong
To the good ol' USA

And now they have a name

Chinook jumping

Leaping

Out of the water

The red bloom

Fallen out of the sky

Fallen out of the sky

Arnold alone in the room
When Frank Brown

Phones from hotel desk
They're on their way up

Tells him Crisman and Smith
Stepped out for a few minutes

Dahl won't talk to anyone

4:30 PM
July 31st

They come right up

Captain Davidson
Short and stocky

Smiling

Very friendly

The long scar
On his face

He and Lt. Brown
Find a chair

Davidson smiles

We have something to tell you
And you're going to love it

FORMATION

Smith and Crisman
Walk in

Davidson takes
A piece of paper

From his pocket

Giggles

Now observe gentlemen

Draws a picture
Of a disc

Almost identical
To one peculiar disc

That has worried Arnold

Different from the rest

Darker

Different shape

Like a crescent

A crescent

This is a drawing
Of one of several photographs

We consider it to be authentic

We just received it at Hamilton Field

Lt. Brown smiles
Nods his head

Face glows

Glows

That's right
It came from Arizona

We have prints at Hamilton Field

But the original negatives
Were flown to Washington DC

Tells Arnold and Smith

If you ever get down
To Hamilton Field

We want you
To call on us

We'll be glad
To have the file opened
So you can see the pictures

Your jaws will drop

They're stunning

Absolutely stunning

Darker

Different shape

Like a crescent

A crescent

For next two and a half hours

Fred Crisman tells
Harold Dahl's story

FORMATION

Hands Brown and Davidson
Some of the fragments

Lying around in a pile
On the floor

Some 25 to 30 pieces

Handle them
While they listen

To Crisman's story

After the session
Cheeseburgers and fries
In the room

Discuss mysterious
Telephone informant

Morello and Lane
Trying to get a story

Almost midnight

Crisman recounts
His own experiences

I saw a craft too

Through the clouds

Brilliant

Not one brilliance

But of many brilliances

Many brilliances

Says he will go home
Get a box of fragments

Bring them down immediately

So they can take them back
To Hamilton Field

But they have lost
Their enthusiasm

Not interested anymore

What happened?

What happened?

They get up

We have to go

Smith and Arnold
Insist they stay the night

Propose two fold down beds
Be brought in

But they'll have none of it

We can't stay

Tomorrow is August 1st

First official day
Of United States Air Force

None of this Army Air Force crap anymore

We're liberated

FORMATION

Every plane
At Hamilton Field

Has to be there
Take part in the maneuvers

Every plane

They flew to Tacoma
In a B-25 bomber

Just gone through
Major overhaul

Two shiny brand new engines

Has to be on flight line
And ready in the morning

Or it's our asses

Arnold and Smith
Feel embarrassed

Like they were dumb victims
Of a silly hoax

But why?

Why?

Standing on the curb
Outside of hotel

Just as Army Command car
Pulls up

So does Fred Crisman

Double parks
1932 blue Ford Roadster

Starts to take a large box
Of Kellogg's Corn Flakes

Out of the trunk
Of his car

Captain Davidson
Tells chauffer

To wait a second

Peers inside the box

Helps Crisman unload the box

Lifts trunk
Of his Command car

Puts it in

Under the street lights

Top of the box
Flapping open

The dark molten lava

The fragments

Whatever they are

They say goodbye

As car pulls away

Arnold shouts

Goodbye and good luck!

FORMATION

Thank you!

Crisman

I'll take you out to the island tomorrow

He drives away

Well, it's out of our hands
Be a relief to get out of here

And how

It's Military Intelligence's problem now

Smithy starts singing a song

A hit by Danny Kaye
About a leaky faucet

Bloop, bleep, bloop, bloop, bleep
The faucet keeps a drippin and I can't sleep
Bleep, bloop, bleep, bloop, bloopbloop, bleep
I guess I never should've ordered clam soup

They start to giggle

Share a smoke

I think we're losing it Smithy

Big toothy grin

Yep, I think you're right

Next morning

Captain Smith
Takes a bath

Singing from the tub

138

Bloop, bleep, bloop, bloop, bleep

They don't have a name
Until now

Flying Saucer Man

Telephone rings

Fred Crisman

Did you hear?

Did you hear
Over the radio?

No. Hear what?

A B-25 exploded
And crashed 20 minutes
After take off

From McChord Field
About 1:30 this morning

I think you and I both know
Who was on that plane

Fallen out of the sky

Fallen out of the sky

★★

What's happening?

What's happening?

Smith calls
McChord Field

FORMATION

Turns white
While he's on the phone

Two of the four men
On the plane

Parachuted to safety

But not Brown
And Davidson

The first casualties
Of the new United States Air Force

First casualties

Arnold calls
Editor Ray Palmer
Evanston, Illinois

First time
He ever speaks to him

Tells him
He'll return the $200

Tells him about the crash

There's a story here
But I don't know up from down anymore

Tells him about the crash

He's not qualified
To investigate this anymore

Much bigger than me
Mr. Palmer

Ken, keep the money
And don't take any of the fragments
On board your plane
Mail them to yourselves
Mail them

Don't take any of the fragments
On board your plane

Calls Crisman

Tell him they
Still want to go down

See his boat

Get out to that island

After they visit Ted Morello
At UP

Tremendously bright flash

Lights up whole cockpit

Whole cockpit

Pulsating

Pulsating

Like a jellyfish

The red bloom

Fish jumping

Skipping on water

They number nine

FORMATION

Flying diagonally

Echelon formation

United Press Building

Just across the street

From the hotel

Ted Morello

Dark man
Five feet seven inches

Motions with his arm
To follow him

Small auditorium

Off to the side
Turns on tape recorder

Words of man
Who parachuted

From the plane

Army man
Who was hitching

A ride with the B-25
Back to California

Just returned
From duty

Allowed a ride
If there is room

The pilot and co-pilot
Strangers to him

So was the engineer

Didn't even know their names

Didn't know their names

Shortly before take off

The pilot and co-pilot

Loaded a corn flakes box

Aboard the plane

A corn flakes box

He noticed it particularly

Because it seemed

Heavy for a box of cereal

For one man to carry

Placed over side compartment

Like a saucer

If you skipped it across the water

The tail of a Chinese kite
Blowing in the wind

Flying saucer

15 to 20 minutes
After take off

FORMATION

Left engine
Catches fire

Catches fire

Pull valve
For emergency firefighting system

For that engine

Doesn't work
Remark that this shouldn't be

Just got a whole makeover

Should work

Should work

Tall co-pilot
Squeezes through doorway

Southern guy

Calmly tells them
To strap on our parachutes

Commands them

Tells him how
To pull the rip cord

When he is sure

He is clear of ship

Make sure you're clear

As he is being
Shoved out of plane

Notices something funny

All happens so fast

Maybe it is just the light
Playing tricks

Could swear that cereal box
Is glowing

Glowing
Like light bulbs inside

Parachute opens
9 to 11 minutes

While floating down
To earth

Watch burning airplane

Burning airplane

Get smaller

Can't see it anymore

Assumes those guys
Got out

Glowing

No one knows why
Brown and Davidson

Didn't evacuate

No box found yet

No fragments

FORMATION

Ted Morello

This whole business
Has gotten out of hand
I am now only interested
In your personal safety

Yes, that has occurred to us

I'll you boys
When an informant can't get
Information in this neck of the woods

Brother, there's something wrong

There's something wrong

Pulsating

Pulsating

Begins spewing forth

What seems like

Confetti

Or thousands
Of newspapers

Glowing
Like light bulbs inside

Go down to the pier
Visit Crisman

Go for that ride
Maury Island

Confetti

Spewing forth

Grayish boat

The North Queen

Small type of
Partially enclosed inboard fishing boat

Doesn't look like
Harbor patrol boat

Inspect

Can see
Where repairs had been done

Smithy whispers to Arnold

Not sure I want to step foot
On this hunk of junk

It's no DC-3

Ask about the photographs

I don't know
What could have happened to them
I can't find them in my office
I looked everywhere

Might be up in his mountain cabin

We can drive up there
And look

We can drive up there

Uh, we'll take a rain check on that

FORMATION

Go down to engine room

Hispanic man
Big mustache

Grease all over him

Remarks to Crisman

Engine don't work

Dead fish
Float everywhere

Silver
Glinting in the sun

The red bloom

Glowing
Like light bulbs inside

Crisman and the mechanic
Go off to the side

And chat

Whispering

The mechanic's having
A hard time

Getting the engine going
It'll take about an hour

Doesn't look like
The engine's been touched

I'll call you
When we're ready

I'll call you

Have lunch in town

Go back to the room

The workers on strike

No elevator

Trudge up the stairs

Flutter and sail

One of the craft

Looked different
From the rest

Darker

Different shape

Like a crescent

A tremendously bright flash

Pulsating

Pulsating

Like a jellyfish

Fallen out of the sky

The Swan Queen

If the vow
Of eternal love is broken

FORMATION

She will remain
A swan forever

Von Rohbart
Deceives Prince Siegfried

He thinks he is dancing
With Odette

But it is Von Rothbart's daughter
Odile

Doesn't know

That he has betrayed her

They dance

Saute

Lifts her

Glitter
Raining down

But it's darker

Darker

Vow of eternal love
Is broken

Broken

A terrible spell

They make no sound

Bloop, bleep, bloop, bloop, bleep
I guess I never should've ordered clam soup

Glows
Like light bulbs inside

Puffing Chesterfields

Phone rings

Ted Morello

Mysterious informant

Says Smith will be called
To Wright-Patterson Field
Dayton, Ohio

To be interrogated

Military Intelligence

Kenneth Arnold's plane
Had been shot at

Shot at

And the B-25 bomber
Was shot down by a 20mm cannon

You're in danger

Frankly, we don't know
What you saw

We don't know what they are

It's not us

Betrayed her

She will remain
A swan forever

FORMATION

A terrible spell

Decide to heed
Morello's advice

Leave town

But expect
Military Intelligence

To contact them

We should stick around
Another day

We owe it to Brown and Davidson

Calls Doris

You sound upset

Tells her about Brown and Davidson

Those nice fellas
That's horrible
Horrible
Please come home Ken
Let it go

I will

And you'll be in time for Kiska

It's not us

Crisman never calls

They call him

No answer

Goes downstairs
To buy cigarettes
At newsstand

Buys final edition
Of Tacoma Times

SABOTAGE HINTED IN CRASH
OF ARMY BOMBER AT KELSO

Lights a Chesterfield

Puffs

Puffs

And sub-headline

Plane May Hold Flying Disc Secret

**May have been shot down
To prevent shipment**

**Of flying disc fragments
To Hamilton Field, California
For analysis**

**Platter fragments
Were loaded aboard
A B25 at McChord Field**

Call Crisman again

Nothing

Attempt to reach
Harold Dahl

No answer

FORMATION

No answer

Dragnet of calls
To movie theaters

And cafes

Places they think
Dahl might frequent

Find him

Hiding in a movie theater

BLUE SKIES

Starring
Bing Crosby and Fred Astaire

All day

Over and over again

Comes to the hotel

Terrified

Tells them Crisman
Left a message

Going to be gone
For a few days

Morello calls

Mysterious telephone informant:

Fred Crisman
Has boarded Army bomber
That afternoon

Being flown
To Alaska

Call McChord Field

Indeed an Army bomber
Did take off

For Alaska

Can't get passenger list

The three of them confused

Confused

Light shines on them
Through the clouds

They are brilliant

Not one brilliance

But of many brilliances

All rise

And disappear

They sit Dahl down

Tell him firmly

That he can't vanish
On them again

Military Intelligence

Or either McChord Field
Or Hamilton Field

FORMATION

Will be debriefing them soon

We were the last people
To see Brown and Davidson alive

They have to
Want to talk to us

-Okay
- I don't like it
- But I'll stick around

Phone rings

Ted Morello

Tried in every conceivable way
To find out

Who the mysterious informant is

Trace his calls

Couldn't

And we're good at that

Find out information
From McChord Field

Drew a blank

We have informants
Who practically smell the runways for news
That B-25 was under armed guard
Every minute
It was at the field

Every minute

Why?

He is concerned for their welfare

I think you're nice fellows
I don't want to see
Anything happen to you
If you can prevent it

All rise

And disappear

Out to sea

What the hell just happened?

★★

They do not hear
From Military Intelligence

Smithy calls
McChord Fields

Talks to someone there
In the Intelligence Division

Tells them
Exactly where they are

If they want to meet them

Discouraged look
On his face

Want someone to talk to

We're sitting on a pile of information

FORMATION

But no one seems
To want to talk them

Why?
Why are we like a couple of dead ducks?
Two people were just killed

No one wants to give us the time of day

Guests arrive
At the palace

Six princesses
Presented to Prince Siegfried

One of whom
His mother hopes

He will choose
As a bride

Von Rothbart
Arrives in disguise

With his enchantress daughter
Odile

The Black Swan

Transformed

She appears
Identical to Odette

Mistakes Odile
For Odette

The Black Swan
For the Swan Queen

Has eyes only for her

Only for her

Dances with Odile

Leaps

The Black Swan

Dark glitter

Rains down
On them

Tilt of her chim

An exaltation

Dark glitter

Von Rothbart
Shows Siegfried

Magical vision
Of Odette

Realizes his mistake

But too late

Too late

Grief stricken

She will remain
A swan forever

A swan forever

A terrible spell

FORMATION

They don't know
If any of the fragments

Worth sending home

Give up trying to get
To Maury Island

Believe Dahl's story true
In many respects

But outside of fragments
On the floor

Can't prove a thing

Not a thing

What is it
That they are seeing

No motors

Propellers

Any visible signs
Of propulsion

They make no sound

No sound

Begins spewing forth

What seems like

Confetti

Flutters to earth

Fluttering

Lights up the bay

Steam rises from the water

Afternoon
Dahl stops by

Brief visit
Not much to say

Paces

Smokes

Invites them to breakfast
Next morning

Small café
Along main highway

Seattle to Portland

Eastern outskirts
Of Tacoma

Bacon and eggs

Smithy –

I have to get back
To my airline runs
Or I'm going to be out of a job

Dahl's secretary
Jeanie with him

Doesn't smile
Or say much

FORMATION

Smithy suddenly gets up
Goes to the pay phone

Makes a call

Returns to the booth

I'm going to be gone
For about an hour Ken
I'm sorry
I can't tell you why

Tells Arnold
That when he returns to the hotel

Stay in the room

And wait for him

Wait for Smithy

Don't leave the room
Under any circumstances

Any circumstances

Lock the door

Will be back
To the hotel

Not later than noon

Not later than noon

You've got to trust me
Don't worry about me
Coming up missing
That's not going to happen

Not going to happen

But six men

Are now down to three

And Dahl's already shaky

Shaky

Going to crack

Ok Smithy
I'll expect you at noon

I'll do exactly
As you say

Carry out his orders

Back to the hotel room

Lock the door

Paces

Smokes

Smoke rings

Wiping his eyes

Noon

!2:30

1 pm

Still no Smithy

Paces

FORMATION

Smokes

Bloop, bleep, bloop, bloop, beep
The faucet keeps a dripin and I can't sleep

It does not belong
To the good ol' USA

The red bloom

Pulsating

Falling out of the sky

Dead fish
Float everywhere

Silver
Glinting in the sun

Bleep bloop bleep bloop bloopbloop bleep
I guess I never should've ordered clam soup

2 pm

Knock on the door

Smithy that you?

Yes

Opens door

With him is
A military man

Major Sander
S-2 Army Intelligence
McChord Field

Ken, I'll tell you where I was
And what I did

Ok

Phoned McChord Field
From the café
Told Major Sander
That needed to see him immediately
I drove out to the base
I didn't tell you where I was going
Or whom I was seeing
For the simple reason
That I wanted to tell my story

And you need to tell him yours

Major Sander can compare

The interpretation of events

That's swell Smithy
Boy am I glad to see you!

Major Sander
Gray hair
5 foot eleven

Pleasant smile
Blue eyes

Dart back and forth
Doesn't miss a beat

Soft voice
Takes a chair

Over by the window

FORMATION

Starts listening
To Arnold's story

Tremendously bright flash

So brilliant

Lights up whole cockpit

Whole cockpit

Pulsating

Pulsating

They number nine

Flying diagonally

Echelon formation

Draw a picture
Of a disc

Different from the rest

Darker

Different shape

Like a crescent

A crescent

We consider it to be authentic

Major Sander quiet

Smiles to himself

Clears his throat

Crosses his arms

Taps his foot

**Gentlemen
I hate to tell you this**

**But you are victims
Of a hoax**

What about the B-25?
Not a good first day for the United States Air Force

**What about the B-25?
It was an accident**

**Still under investigation
But seems to be no sign of foul play**

There was no sign of any fragments

This is all not properly investigated yet

Could take weeks

**Do not discuss this matter
With anyone**

**Any further
Any more**

In approximately two weeks

**Through this office
Of S-2 Military Intelligence**

**An explanation
Will be forthcoming**

To each of you privately

FORMATION

Loud sigh

Picks up some fragments

Turns them over
In his hands

Would have them analyzed
For the sake of being thorough

Betrayed

Realizing his mistake

But too late

Grief stricken

She will remain
A swan forever

A swan forever

Rushes to the lake

She is distraught
At his betrayal

Resigned to death

A terrible spell

He wants to
Take them for a ride

I'm going to show you
Thousands of tons
Of this stuff

**I can assure
It's not from any flying discs**

Sure, we would love to see it

Starts wrapping fragments
In hotel towel

Intention of taking with him

Bundled in towels

I'd sure like to keep one as an ashtray
Like a souvenir

Me too

Smiles

Nods

**Gentlemen,
I need every piece**

**We don't want to overlook
Even one piece**

I need every piece

Every piece

Puts his hand out
For the souvenirs

Hmm

Proceeds to wrap up
Everything in a bundle

Searches the room

FORMATION

Under the bed

Finds another fragment

Have to be thorough

They carry the bundles
Downstairs to his car

Opens trunk

Places wrapped fragments
In the trunk

*I think the hotel is
Going to be a short a few towels*

Stares at him

Darting eyes

Smiles

Yes indeed they are

Whispers to Smithy

*We should have mailed some home
When we had the chance*

Big, toothy grin

Not convinced they would have made it pal

Glows
Like light bulbs inside

Dead fish
Float everywhere

Silver
Glinting in the sun

The bloom

Pulsating

Pulsating

Fallen out of the sky

Motions for them
To get in the car

Smithy and Arnold
Look at each other

A nice scenic car ride boys

Shrug

Get in

Drive out to the point
Of the peninsula

Large sign
TACOMA SMELTING COMPANY

Drive along road
Into the grounds

Piles of lava-like
Smelter slag

At first glance
Identical to the fragments

At first glance

FORMATION

Stops the car

To get out

To look at smelter slag

Drive down a side road
Among piles of slag

They all get out

Smithy and Arnold

Pick up pieces

Hold them

Examine

Rub them

They've held the fragments
In the room

Many times

Many times

Smithy looks at Arnold

Big toothy grin

Shakes his head

Nope

But they keep quiet

The Major stares
At Smithy and Arnold

Darting eyes

Let's all have smoke

They light up

He puffs

Exhales

**See Gentlemen
They're just lava rocks**

**That's all
It was just a simple rouse**

That's all

They get back in the car

Thanks for setting us straight Major
We feel relieved

Well I am glad I could be of help

Still let's keep this all quiet, yes?

We won't talk about it anymore

With anyone

With anyone, ok?

Silence

No motors

Propellers

Any visible signs
Of propulsion

FORMATION

They make no sound

No sound

Begins spewing forth

What seems like

Confetti

Or thousands
Of newspapers

When they get
Back to the hotel

Pack up their suitcases

And check out

Let's get out of this insanity

I second that motion

Sighs of relief

They intend to go
Directly to Barry's Airport

When they get
Into Smithy's car

Arnold suggests
They say goodbye to Dahl

I'd like to give him a bear hug

Tell him everything will be alright

Seems sincere

I feel sorry for him

And I'm sorry
We can't figure it all out

We should at least say good bye

Of course you're right Ken

Mentioned that we was going
To work all day

Some book work
At his secretary's house

Make a quick run there

I know exactly where that house is
I was paying attention
Only a ten minute ride

Has Smithy take
Exactly the same route

Arrive at the little white house
On the corner

Arnold's jaw drops

Gets out of the car

Walks up same crooked sidewalk

Shit a brick! No!
It can't be!

It can't be!

Smithy looks at Arnold
Puzzled

FORMATION

What's the matter?

The house is the same
In every respect

Same location
Where he went

The first night

The house is empty

Completely empty

Probably the wrong house Ken
They look a lot alike around here
Looks like no one's been here for years

No Smithy
It's the same house

It's the same house

I know it is

Steps up to the porch

Same squeak

Screen door ajar

The stain glass window
With the orchid

Green and red

Same door knob

Oblong little
Grape insignia

The same

Door of dark mahogany

The same

Is locked

But peers inside

Same oak floor

Dust

Everything empty

Cobwebs

Years of cobwebs

Can see
Markings on the floor

Where the piano was

But it was there

I can tell

The radio is gone

Lights a Chesterfield

Puffs

Shakes his head

Takes a walk
Around the side

FORMATION

The aerial is still there
And the base

Peers in the windows

Cobwebs

Years of cobwebs

Rooms all the same

And the green kitchen

Mumbles to himself

Incredible!
Absolutely incredible!

You ok buddy?

No, I think I'm losing it Smithy
Like really losing it

My God

My God

No one's been here for years Ken

★★

Pull up to Barry's Airport

In the terminal
They hear on the radio

More news about the
C-46 Marine Transport

That disappeared in December

Crashed into the face

Of a sheer 3,000 foot cliff

Ranger's report

Plane exploded

Scattered wreckage

And personnel over a wide area

32 souls abroad

Parents who waited
At the foot of the trail

Receive news
Of the discovery calmly

First bodies found
Along with a section
Of the plane

Fulfillment of a dream

But far too treacherous

To attempt any recovery

So with approval
Of the families

The men are left
To rest in peace forever

Where last they lay already

Partially entombed

Glacial ice

FORMATION

Highest slope of the mountain

To rest in peace forever

Fulfillment of a dream

From the terminal

Arnold attempts to call Harold Dahl

Disconnected

Calls the operator

Harold Dahl

Or HA Dahl

No listing

Has never been such a listing

Never been

Ok, we're out of here

Flying Saucer Man

Arnold suggests

That Smithy and he

Inspect his ship

From nose to tail

CallAir A-2 mountain plane

125 horsepower Lycoming engine

Climbs 1000 feet a minute
Fully loaded
Range of 500 miles

You're good to go Ken

One last smoke

Bloop, bleep, bloop, bloop, bleep

They chuckle

Big toothy grin

Starts the engine

Warms it up good

Checks both his magnetos

At full throttle

Gas lines

Fuel valves

Everything in perfect order

Though late in day

Only a four hour flight
To Boise

I'm coming home Kiska

I'm coming home

Shoves throttle
Clear to the instrument panel

Takes off

FORMATION

Circles airport

Can see the little figure

Of Big Smithy

Waving at him

Walking back to his car

Waving

Climb to eight thousand feet

His movie camera at hand

Just in case

Just in case

They don't have a name
Until now

Flying Saucer Man

The air so smooth today

So smooth

And clear

Clear as crystal

A pleasure to fly

I'm still a lucky man

A pleasure to fly

Odette forgives Siegfried

For his betrayal

Affirm their love

They dance

Saute

Other worldy

Magical

Her soft arms

Graceful back

Delicate feet

Leaps light
And sharp

Affirm their love

Von Rothbart appears

Insists that Siegfried
Fulfill his pledge

To marry Odile

Evil enchantress daughter

Black Swan

After which

Odette will be transformed
Into a swan forever

A swan forever

A terrible spell

FORMATION

Crosses the Cascades

Let down
Over the Columbia River

With intention
Of landing at Pendleton

Gas her up

Everything running smoothly

A pleasure to fly

Lands at Pendleton

Boys there gas up his ship

Gets out of cockpit

To stretch his legs

Signs credit slip

Full tank of gas

Ready to take off again

For home

Home

Shoves the throttle

Engine roars

Off the ground

50 foot altitude

Engine stops cold

Stops cold

Stalls

As if every piston
Frozen solid

Not enough speed
To sustain

For normal landing

Stops cold

Shit!

Straight ahead

No power

No lift

Put her down

Drive plane
Straight at the ground

Within 10 feet of runway

Come back on the stick

As fast as he can

Attempt to level off

Comes through

Sets her down

Doesn't know what happened

FORMATION

Unhurt

Jumps out of cockpit

Runs around

To front of plane

Turns propeller

Loose and easy

Not the problem

People run over

To see what happened

You ok?
You ok?

I'm fine

Wants to see
If the engine will start again

Figures this would happen

Climbs back into cockpit

What caused the engine to stop?

Fuel valve shut off

Fuel valve

I must have done it

It was fine in Tacoma

Turns it back on

One of the fellows

Swings the propeller

Engine starts immediately

And smoothly

Takes off again

I'm coming home Kiska

This time for real

The air smooth

And clear

Coming home

Keeps the movie camera
At hand

Just in case

Just in case

Plies, pirouettes
And poise

Floor formations

Odette and Siegfried
Drown themselves in the lake

To preserve their love forever

As they descend

Glitter rains down

FORMATION

Glitter

Drown themselves

To preserve their love forever

They don't have a name
Until now

A tremendously bright flash

Lights up the surface
Of his aircraft

Tremendously bright flash

Lights up whole cockpit

Whole cockpit

Pulsating

Pulsating

Blue-white flashes emit
From the center

Of their surfaces

Similar in pulsation
And rhythm and beating

Of the human heart

Drown themselves

To preserve their love forever

Glitter raining down

The air so smooth today

So smooth

And clear

Blue skies